Mathematical Games for One or Two

Mathematical Games

for One or Two

by Mannis Charosh
illustrated by Lois Ehlert

Thomas Y. Crowell Company
New York

YOUNG MATH BOOKS

Edited by Dr. Max Beberman, Director of the Committee on
School Mathematics Projects, University of Illinois

BIGGER AND SMALLER
by Robert Froman

CIRCLES
by Mindel and Harry Sitomer

COMPUTERS
by Jane Jonas Srivastava

THE ELLIPSE
by Mannis Charosh

ESTIMATION
by Charles F. Linn

FRACTIONS ARE PARTS OF THINGS
by J. Richard Dennis

GRAPH GAMES
by Frédérique and Papy

LINES, SEGMENTS, POLYGONS
by Mindel and Harry Sitomer

LONG, SHORT, HIGH, LOW, THIN, WIDE
by James T. Fey

MATHEMATICAL GAMES FOR ONE OR TWO
by Mannis Charosh

ODDS AND EVENS
by Thomas C. O'Brien

PROBABILITY
by Charles F. Linn

RIGHT ANGLES:
PAPER-FOLDING GEOMETRY
by Jo Phillips

RUBBER BANDS, BASEBALLS AND
DOUGHNUTS:
A BOOK ABOUT TOPOLOGY
by Robert Froman

STRAIGHT LINES, PARALLEL LINES,
PERPENDICULAR LINES
by Mannis Charosh

WEIGHING & BALANCING
by Jane Jonas Srivastava

WHAT IS SYMMETRY?
by Mindel and Harry Sitomer

Edited by Dorothy Bloomfield, Mathematics Specialist,
Bank Street College of Education

VENN DIAGRAMS *by Robert Froman*

L. C. Card 74-187934
ISBN 0-690-52324-6
0-690-52325-4 (LB)

2   3   4   5   6   7   8   9   10

Mathematical Games
for One or Two

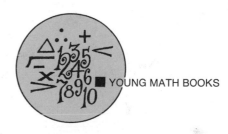 YOUNG MATH BOOKS

THIS IS ONE OF CROWELL'S
YOUNG MATH BOOKS

Here are some mathematical games. The first three can be played by yourself. The last three can be played with a friend. Some are played with cards that have numbers on them. Others are played with small things like checkers or marbles. Many people like the kind of thinking that is needed to play these games. See whether you do.

Pyramid Games for One Player

First Pyramid Game

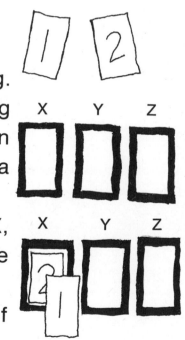

Cut out two pieces of thin cardboard or oaktag. The pieces should be about the same size as playing cards. Write the numerals 1 on one card and 2 on the other. Or you can take an ace and a 2 from a deck of playing cards. The ace counts as 1.

Next, on a piece of paper draw three spaces, X, Y, Z, next to each other. Make each space a little bigger than the size of a card.

Put the 2 in space X and put the 1 on top of the 2.

You play the game by moving the top card on any space to the top of any other space. But you may not put a card with a larger number on top of a card with a smaller number. You may put a 1 on top of a 2. But you may not put a 2 on top of a 1.

Let's call a 1 on top of a 2 a TWO-CARD PYRAMID. In later games, we will call a 1 on top of a 2 on top of a 3 a THREE-CARD PYRAMID, and so on.

The object of the first game is to move the two-card pyramid from space X to space Z. Try to do it in as few moves as you can. All three spaces may be used. Keep a record of the number of moves you make. Let's try it.

First put the 1 in space Z.

Next put the 2 in space Y.

Then put the 1 on the 2.

The two-card pyramid is now in space Y. But we want it in space Z.

Now move the 1 to space X.

Next move the 2 to space Z.

Then put the 1 on the 2.

The pyramid is now in space Z. That took six moves.

4

5

Let's begin again and see if we can do it in fewer moves.

First put the 1 in space Y, not Z as before.

Next put the 2 in space Z

Then put the 1 on top of the 2.

We have moved the two-card pyramid from space X to space Z in just three moves.

YOU CAN ALWAYS MOVE A TWO-CARD PYRAMID FROM ONE SPACE TO ANY OTHER SPACE IN THREE MOVES.

We have learned something about working a problem that has more than one way to begin. Begin in any way. If it doesn't work start over with another way.

X   Y   Z

Second Pyramid Game

You will make the game a little harder if you add a 3 to the 1 and 2. Make a three-card pyramid in space X. Remember that you should have the 1 on top of the 2 on top of the 3.

The object of this game is to move the three-card pyramid from space X to space Z.

Should you begin by moving the 1 to space Y or to Z? Since there are two ways to begin, try one. Move the 1 to space Y. Next move the 2 to space Z. Then put the 1 on top of the 2. If you move the 3 to space Y, you can move the two-card pyramid from space Z to space Y in three more moves. But you want the three-card pyramid in space Z. Try a new start.

See if you can do the whole thing yourself. If you have to, look at the answer on the next page. How many steps did it take you? Can you do it in fewer steps?

X Y Z

Answer to the Second Pyramid Game

Move the 1 to space Z. Put the 2 in space Y. Put the 1 on top of the 2. Move the 3 to space Z. Move the 1 to space X. Put the 2 on top of the 3. Then put the 1 on top of the 2. It took seven moves to move the three-card pyramid from space X to space Z.

YOU CAN ALWAYS MOVE A THREE-CARD PYRAMID FROM ONE SPACE TO ANY OTHER SPACE IN SEVEN MOVES.

An easy way to remember how to do this Pyramid Game is to break it up into three parts: First, move the two-card pyramid to the space that will not be the last one. This takes three moves. Second, move the 3 to the last space. This takes one move. Third, move the two-card pyramid to the top of the 3. This takes three more moves. The three parts should take 3 + 1 + 3, or seven moves.

You can, of course, make the game harder by starting with four cards, five cards, and so on. With four cards it should take 7 + 1 + 7, or fifteen moves to move the pyramid from space X to space Z.

Shifting Games for One Player

First Shifting Game

You play this game with cards 1 (or ace), 2, and 3. On a piece of paper draw four spaces, two next to each other, and two under them.

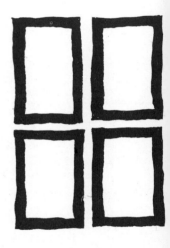

Put the 3 in the upper left space. Then put the 1 in the upper right space. And then put the 2 in the lower left space. You play the game by moving any card up or down or right or left into an empty space. You may begin by moving the 1 down or the 2 to the right. You really do not have to say "down" or "right." Do you see why?

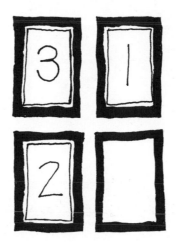

The object of the game is to move the cards one at a time into the empty spaces so that you end up with them in the order 1, 2, 3.

Here is one way of doing it. Move the 2, 3, 1, 2 in that order.

Second Shifting Game

This is a little harder. We will use a 1, 2, 3, 4, and 5.

On a piece of paper draw three spaces next to each other, and three more spaces under those. Put the 4 in the upper left space. Put the 3 at its right. Then put the 5 in the upper right space. Now put the 2 under the 4 and the 1 under the 3.

The object of the game is to move the cards one at a time into empty spaces so that you end up with them in the order 1, 2, 3, 4, 5.

Try it yourself. Remember what you learned in the Pyramid Games. If one way doesn't work, try another. There are many ways of choosing moves. Can you finish the game in eight moves? If not, look at the answer on page 14.

Answer to the Second Shifting Game

Move in turn: 5, 3, 1, 2, 4, 1, 2, 5.

You can make up other games with the same five cards and six spaces. First put the cards in the right order: 1, 2, 3, 4, 5. Then move the cards around into spaces to mix them up. Copy down the order you end with. Now try to bring back the first order: 1, 2, 3, 4, 5.

You might think it will be easier to mix up the cards first and then put them down in any order. But in some cases you may find that you can get the cards back only to the order 1, 2, 3, 5, 4. You will not be able to get back to the right order.

You can make many more games by adding more cards and spaces. You can draw nine spaces: three under three under three, and use cards 1, 2, 3, 4, 5, 6, 7, and 8. Put the cards in that order. Mix them up by moving them in any way that you wish in the spaces. Then try to move them back into the order you began with.

Checker Games for One Player

First Checker Game

To play this game you will need a red checker, a black checker, and a checkerboard. If you don't have a checkerboard, you can draw three squares in a row on a piece of paper. If you don't have  checkers, you can use poker chips, bottle caps, or coins.

Put the black checker in the lower left-hand square. Skip the next square to the right and put a red checker in the third square to the right.

In the game, the black checker may move only to the right. The red checker may move only to the left. A checker can move into an empty square, or it can jump over a different-colored checker.

The object of the game is to end up with the red checker where the black one is, and the black checker where the red one is.

You will easily find the answer: Black moves, Red jumps, Black moves.

You can make the game harder by using more checkers and more squares.

Try these games. Begin with Black in each game.

Second Checker Game

Start with this:

End with this:

Third Checker Game

Start with this:

End with this:

Fourth Checker Game

Start with this:

End with this:

Fifth Checker Game

Start with this:

End with this:

The answers are on the next page.

Answers to the Checker Games

Second Checker Game: Black moves, Red jumps, Black moves, Black jumps, Red moves.

Third Checker Game: Black moves, Red jumps, Red moves (if Black moves here it will not work; try it), Black jumps, Black jumps, Red moves, Red jumps, Black moves.

Fourth Checker Game: Black moves, Red jumps, Red moves, Black jumps, Black jumps, Black moves (look at the order of the colors now: black, red, black, red, black), Red jumps, Red jumps, Black moves, Black jumps, Red moves.

Fifth Checker Game: Black moves, Red jumps, Red moves, Black jumps, Black jumps, Black moves (again, look at the order of the colors), Red jumps, Red jumps, Red jumps, Black moves, Black jumps, Black jumps, Red moves, Red jumps, Black moves.

Take-Away Games for Two Players

First Take-Away Game

Put three small things, such as checkers or marbles, on a table. Each player in turn must take away one or two checkers. The one who takes away the last checker is the winner. Who should win, the first player or the second player?

If the first player takes one, the second player wins by taking away the other two. If the first player takes two, the second player wins by taking the last checker.

IN A GAME WITH THREE THINGS, THE SECOND PLAYER WINS.

Second Take-Away Game

If there are four checkers on the table, who should win? If the first player takes away one checker, he should win. That is because he leaves three things. This is now the same as the first game. The one who began in the first game had to lose. The second player is now beginning a game like the first game. He must lose.

Third Take-Away Game

If there are six checkers on the table, who should win? This time the first player should not win. If he takes away one checker, the second player can win by taking two checkers. If the first player takes two checkers, the second player can win by taking one checker. Each time the second player leaves three checkers, as in the first game.

IN A GAME WITH SIX THINGS, THE SECOND PLAYER SHOULD WIN.

Now try games beginning with five, seven, eight, nine, ten, or more things. You will find that the second player should win only if there are three, six, nine things, and so on. At all other times the first player should win.

Nim - a Game for Two Players

In these games two piles of things, such as tooth-picks or marbles, are put on a table. The players take turns. Each player takes as many things as he wishes from just one of the piles. He may take them all if he wishes. The player who takes the last thing wins the game.

First Nim Game

The easiest game to play is one in which there is only one thing in each pile. Do you see that the second player must win?

Second Nim Game

If there are two things in each pile, who should win? The second player should win by doing just what the first player does. If the first player takes one thing from one pile, the second player should take one from the other pile. This game is now the same as the first game. We saw in that game that the second player wins. If the first player takes both things from one pile, the second player wins by taking both things from the other pile.

Third Nim Game

If there are three things in each pile, who should win? Again the second player should win by doing just what the first player does. Try it.

IF THE TWO PILES HAVE THE SAME NUMBER OF THINGS, THE SECOND PLAYER CAN WIN BY DOING JUST WHAT THE FIRST PLAYER DOES.

Fourth Nim Game

If one pile has five things and the other has three things, who should win? The first player should win by taking two things from the first pile. This is because the game will then be the same as the third Nim game.

IF THE TWO PILES HAVE DIFFERENT NUMBERS OF THINGS IN THEM, THE FIRST PLAYER CAN WIN BY MAKING THE NUMBER OF THINGS IN THE TWO PILES THE SAME.

A Game for Magicians

First Magic Trick

This is more of a trick than a game.

Put cards with numbers on them in three rows as shown below.

If you are the magician, ask a friend to think of a number from 1 (Ace) to 7, but not to tell you what it is.

Ask him whether that number is in row A, then in row B, then in row C. From his answers you can figure out the number he is thinking of. You can even turn your back and do this trick.

Suppose he says no for row A, yes for row B, and yes for row C. What number is he thinking of?

The only number that is in both rows B and C is 6. That must be his number.

There is an easy way of knowing this even if your back is turned. Just remember the top number of each row: 1, 2, 4. Since your friend said yes for the second and third rows, add the second and third top numbers. This gives you 2 + 4 = 6.

This will always work because the rows are made so that each number is put only in the rows whose top numbers add up to that number.

Second Magic Trick

If you are good at addition you can have more numbers to choose from. On a piece of paper write numbers in four rows as shown below:

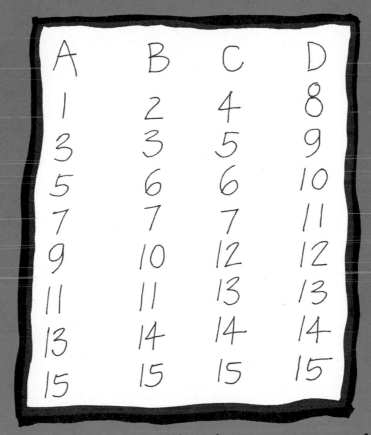

A	B	C	D
1	2	4	8
3	3	5	9
5	6	6	10
7	7	7	11
9	10	12	12
11	11	13	13
13	14	14	14
15	15	15	15

For example, if your friend answers yes for rows A, C, and D, add the top numbers of those rows. You will get: 1 + 4 + 8 = 13. The number he is thinking of is 13.

ABOUT THE AUTHOR

Mannis Charosh has always been interested in mathematical puzzles and games. He is also a chess enthusiast and an award-winning composer of chess problems.

Mr. Charosh has taught mathematics to high school students for many years. The author of THE ELLIPSE and STRAIGHT LINES, PARALLEL LINES, PERPENDICULAR LINES, two other books in Crowell's Young Math series, Mr. Charosh has also written other books, filmstrips, and motion picture narrations about mathematics and the teaching of mathematics.

He now lives with his wife in Brooklyn, New York—where he has lived all of his life.

ABOUT THE ILLUSTRATOR

In MATHEMATICAL GAMES FOR ONE OR TWO Lois Ehlert wanted to illustrate the ideas in a very simple, direct way. "Since the brush couldn't make little marks, only the important parts of the animals emerged. Here are the card shark and the smart fox—but are they really good at math games? For me they are jokes; I hope they will make you giggle, too!"

Miss Ehlert has illustrated many books and has won numerous awards for her artwork. She has also taught art classes and designed clothes, banners, puppets, toys, and games for children.

Lois Ehlert lives in her native state of Wisconsin with her husband, John Reiss, who is also an artist.